Made in the USA
Las Vegas, NV
08 July 2024

92026965R00015